# PHOTOGRAPHY & IMAGING YEARBOOK 2001

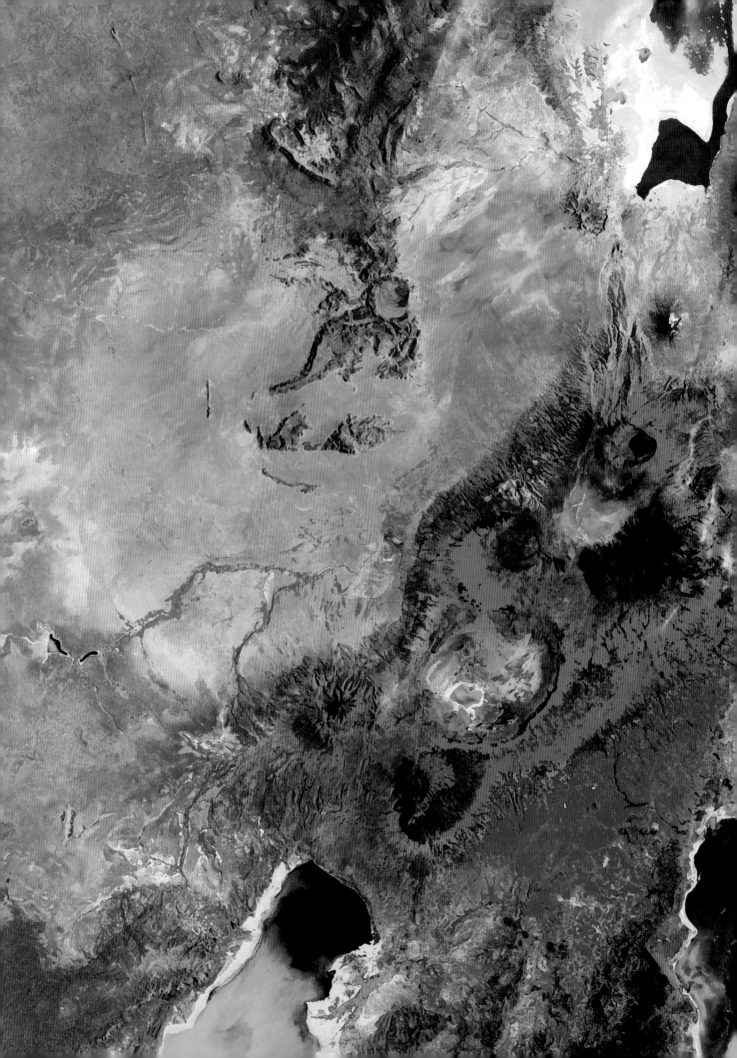

# PHOTOGRAPHY & IMAGING YEARBOOK 2001

PICTURE EDITOR
## Chris Hinterobermaier

DESIGNER
## Grant Bradford

FOUNTAIN PRESS

# PHOTOGRAPHY & IMAGING YEARBOOK 2001

Published by
**FOUNTAIN PRESS**
Newpro UK Limited
Old Sawmills Road
Faringdon
Oxfordshire SN7 7DS
England

Picture Editor
**CHRIS HINTEROBERMAIER**

Designed by
**GRANT BRADFORD**
Design Consultants
Tunbridge Wells, Kent

Reproduction
**NEW CENTURY COLOUR**
Hong Kong

Printed by
**SUPREME PUBLISHING
SERVICES**

© Fountain Press 2000
ISBN 0 86343 378 2

Title page image by Stuart Black
Ngorongoro Conservation Area
and Serengeti Plain, Tanzania

# CONTENTS

Introduction 6

## PORTFOLIOS

### Francisco Hidalgo
VENICE – REFLECTIONS OF A CITY  8

### Simon Marsden
THE SILENT IMAGE  24

### International Portfolio
HOMAGE TO THE GREAT PAINTERS  40

### Rosemary Calvert
BOTANIX  56

### Florian Stöllinger
ENCLOSURES  66

### Hannes Kutzler
BEYOND REALITY  84

## INTERNATIONAL GALLERY

INDEX OF PHOTOGRAPHERS  90

PHOTOGRAPHS 91-253

# INTRODUCTION

The beginning of a new millennium seems an especially appropriate time to reassess, to rethink, and, maybe, to reinvent. A few years from now the way we lead our lives will probably be very different including how we make and display our photographs. Or should I say 'images'?

Five years ago, few photographers would have sat in front of a computer and worked digitally, to produce pictures. Those that did probably already had a keen interest in computers or were working commercially producing images impossible to achieve by conventional photographic techniques.

But with the huge boom in home computer sales and the advent of affordable, sophisticated image-manipulation software, that has changed forever and increasing numbers of keen photographers appreciate the advantages of digitising their images.

Currently, the majority of photographers take their pictures using sensitised film which is processed chemically. The resulting images are then digitised by a scanner and once pictures are available to the computer, they can be manipulated in a wide variety of ways. Many of the shackles that have previously restricted photographers have been shaken off. Flawed pictures can be corrected, family snapshots can be dispatched instantly around the globe via the internet and, most importantly, there are no longer any boundaries to creativity.

But there is more. Many people are taking the whole process a stage further and, to use the jargon, are 'capturing' pictures digitally. Sales of digital cameras are booming, and no wonder. You never have to buy a roll of film or pay for processing ever again and you get to see the picture seconds after taking them. If the shot is no good, it is a simple matter to erase it and reshoot.

There remains a quality gap between digital and film cameras in favour of the latter but that is narrowing rapidly. Advances are fast and frequent and yes ultimately I see a filmless future. In five, ten or twenty years? Who knows. For many camera users, I suspect it will be sooner rather than later.

But having seen a totally digital future, I would like to put on record that I am not a digital missionary. My role, professionally and personally, is not to convert photographers to this new fangled digital thing. On the contrary. I simply wish to highlight the danger of photographers burying their heads in the sand and letting this new technology and all the opportunities it brings bypass them. Rationality, in these fast-moving times, is an important quality.

Which brings me back to my opening call to reassess, rethink and reinvent. I believe we should all look at what is available and then make considered, informed, rational decisions on how to use what is there to make better pictures. And, unlike a few years ago, we need to go through this process more and more frequently.

This soul-searching process is one I have recently gone through. The bottom line is that I remain firmly entrenched in the conventional-imaging camp. I like using film, I enjoy doing my own processing and I like battling in a chemical darkroom. Moreover, I prefer the quality of a well-crafted black and white print compared with that from an inkjet printer. As for my computer, it is reserved for archiving my best shots and writing them onto CD. To me it is the perfect merger of two very different technologies that make my passion for photography more rewarding.

Admittedly, my conclusions are far from ground-breaking and probably twelve months from now I might have swopped my wet darkroom for a completely digital version, or even scrapped the computer completely and taken up sun printing. Who knows? Whatever the future holds, I feel much happier about my photography having taken time out to consider the options.

The Photography Yearbook has just been through the same re-invention process, hence the change in its title which now includes the word 'Imaging'. It is a recognition that photography is much more than drawing with light.

This is a hugely significant and brave step for a book that has been published annually since 1935 (the war years excluded). Looking through its wide variety of images and creative approaches, this year's edition is the best I have seen for many a year.

There is something for everybody and the quality is of the highest order. Each turn of the page brings delight, surprise and inspiration. However each image is produced, the final result is worth looking at and this, I feel, should be the ambition of every photographer.

William Cheung FRPS Editor, Practical Photography

# VENICE
## REFLECTIONS OF A CITY

### Photographs by
### FRANCISCO HIDALGO

Francisco Hidalgo is one of the legends of twentieth century photography. A virtuoso of the camera, his images have been exhibited internationally and published in many books and magazines.

The city has been a focus for Hidalgo who has now turned his attention to the most magical of all cities – VENICE. Hidalgo captures the atmosphere and colour of Venice with this impressionistic images of buildings, water and people.

A unique feature of Hidalgo's photographs is that he makes his images totally in camera by using multiple exposures, deliberate camera movement, filters and other manual effects. Hidalgo pushes 35mm equipment to its limits in order to produce ever more dramatic results ,transcending the camera's usual act of recording to create photographs of great power and beauty. He says *"For a photograph to capture a particular atmosphere, I need a certain light, a subtle ambience. It gives me great pleasure to use the first light of day by rising early as sometimes, filtering through the haze, the sun creates a strange, magical aura".*

Hidalgo has visited Venice many times particularly during the annual carnival, which he loves to photograph. This portfolio contains some of the photographs from his forthcoming book VENICE to be published by Fountain Press.

'those azure, fathomless depths of crystal mystery,
on which the swiftness of the gondola floats'

RUSKIN

*'Underneath Day's azure eyes Ocean's nursling Venice lies,'*
**SHELLEY**

'I stood in Venice on the Bridge of Sighs; A palace and a prison on each han

*saw from out the wave her structures rise As from the stroke of the enchanter's wand:'*

BYRON

'She is Venus when she smiles;
But she's Juno when she walks,
And Minerva when she talks

BEN JONSON

'Dreamlike and dim, but glorious, the unnumbered palaces lift their shafts
out of the hollow sea, – pale ranks of motionless flame,'

RUSKIN

*'The pleasant place of all festivity, The revel of the earth, the masque of Italy'*

**BYRON**

# The SILENT IMAGE

## Photographs by
## SIMON MARSDEN

*Photograph by Caroline Marsden*

On my twenty first birthday my father, a keen landscape photographer, gave me an old Leica camera and I became instantly hooked on photography. What intrigued me most was the magic of time and light, and the enigma of 'reality' that these elements conjured up, and over the years I have tried to portray this mystery in my work.

Influenced by a childhood spent in an archaic, rambling haunted mansion in a remote part of the English countryside, I later discovered the works of Edgar Allan Poe, whose romantic poetry and dark tales of decaying gothic mansions and moonlit abbeys seemed to mirror my own photographs. For me these buildings are symbols of a vast stillness, a silence more dominant than man.

I use infrared film for it's ethereal quality. Day is turned into night and nothing in this twilight world is quite as it seems. The texture of the grain produces a timeless quality that lies somewhere between an etching and a photograph. The exposure and developing of the film is just the beginning, the printing is where the real creative process begins. For me photography is far more than just a technical craft, weeks, even months at a time are spent in the darkroom, I try to put all of myself into the finished print.

Our world today is driven by the relentless and all consuming marriage of science and commerce. As a relief from this life of stark realism we turn to beauty and fantasy. I am interested in photographing places where man has left his spiritual mark in less stressful times, in architecture that is both inspirational and lasting, and in landscapes that portray the inherent power of nature. The mystical quality of my photographs reflects an ancient order and attempts to reveal what is eternal.

Simon's photographs have been exhibited widely throughout the world and can be found in numerous important collections. To date six books of his work have been published, most recently BEYOND THE WALL – THE LOST WORLD OF EAST GERMANY. He is presently working on two further titles: VENICE – CITY OF HAUNTING DREAMS AND THE TWILIGHT HOUSE – ILLUSTRATED WORKS FROM CELTIC MASTERS OF THE SUPERNATURAL.

A picture library of his images, THE MARSDEN ARCHIVE, is available for editorial use.
www.marsdenarchive.com   info@marsdenarchive.com

**Knebworth House,
Hertfordshire,
England**

Opposite
**Burg Kriebstein,
Sachsen, Germany**

Moydrum Castle,
Athlone, County
Westmeath, Ireland

Opposite
Castle Bernard,
Bandon, County Cork,
Ireland

27

Statue,
Waddesdon Manor,
Buckinghamshire,
England

Sphinx by Edenhech,
1755, Schloss
Anssouci, Potsdam,
Germany

Mountain & Birds
New Mexico, USA

**Whitby Abbey,
Yorkshire, England**

**Detail on tomb,**
Père Lachaise Cemetery, Paris

Bamburgh Castle,
Northumberland,
England

Graveyard, Whitby,
Yorkshire, England

Schloss Enigerode,
Sachsen-Anhalt,
Germany

**Dunnottar Castle,
Kincardineshire, Scotland**

Opposite

**Dwarf on the shoulders of a peasant by Carl Roder,
Sommerpalais, Greiz, Thüringen, Germany**

Poulnaborne
Dolmen,
The Burren,
County Clare,
Ireland

# HOMAGE

## A TRIBUTE TO THE GREAT MASTERS

## International Portfolio

What would Leonardo, Rembrandt, Monet, Degas or Picasso have created if modern photographic equipment was made available to them? How would they portray their ideas using film instead of paint?

These interesting questions were posed by Hasselblad in a competition to celebrate its fiftieth anniversary and to create a tribute to the great masters, as well as displaying the creative possibilities of photography to a wider audience.

Photographers from 39 countries entered over 5,000 images from which the winners were selected. Many photographers stretched their technical abilities and discovered new ways to use light, filters, lenses and digital software to produce fitting tribute to the artists they had chosen to emulate.

As photography which has become a hobby for millions and a living for professionals around the world continues to expand and develop, it has also become part of the international art market with historic prints by masters of the nineteenth and twentieth centuries fetching increasingly high prices at auction.

The final overall winner of the competition, Bruce Monk from Winnipeg, Canada with his beautiful black and white photographic work of ballet dancers in a fascinating shadow play (page 53) a tribute to Edgar Degas (1834-1917). The jury said of this image *"It breathes sensitivity and music and contains the elements of Ansel Adams' fine art black and white photography with its subtle shadows, highlights and mid-tones"*.

ARMANDO TOMAGRA
ITALY
HOMAGE TO FRANCIS BACON

40

CARLOS CASARIEGO ROZAS
SPAIN
HOMAGE TO FRANCIS BACON

MILAN PAJK
SLOVENIA
HOMAGE TO RÉNÉ MAGRITTE

GRETA BUYSSE
BELGIUM
HOMAGE TO RÉNÉ MAGRITTE

SERGIO BECCARIA/IVANO CATINI/CARLA CINELLI
ITALY
HOMAGE TO RÉNÉ MAGRITTE

THIONG-TOYE MAKI
SWITZERLAND
HOMAGE TO CLAUDE MONET

JUNJI AKIMOTO
JAPAN
HOMAGE TO CLAUDE MONET

CHUCK DRESNER
UNITED STATES
HOMAGE TO CLAUDE MONET

CHIH-WEI WANG
TAIWAN
HOMAGE TO PABLO PICASSO

AGUS ARIADI
INDONESIA
HOMAGE TO PABLO PICASSO

LUO BIN
HONG KONG
HOMAGE TO PABLO PICASSO

LUIS LADRÓN DE GUEVARA LARSEN
CHILE
HOMAGE TO JOAN MIRÓ

PETER RATHMANN
GERMANY
HOMAGE TO
ANDY WARHOL

MAYUMI GINA HARA
JAPAN
HOMAGE TO EDVARD MUNCH

SONG JIN-TEK
MALAYSIA
HOMAGE TO ZHANG DA QIAN

CHIH-HUEI CHANG
TAIWAN
HOMAGE TO DA-CHIAN CHANG

IWAO HATADA
JAPAN
HOMAGE TO EDGAR DEGAS

GIORGIO SKORY
SWITZERLAND
HOMAGE TO
VINCENT VAN GOGH

JOHN-RAY BETTELL
UNITED KINGDOM
HOMAGE TO
GIOVANNI BELLINI

BRUCE MONK
CANADA
HOMAGE TO
EDGAR DEGAS

54

SHIH-CHEN CHAO
TAIWAN
HOMAGE TO SALVADOR DALI

# BOTANIX

## Photographs by
## ROSEMARY CALVERT

Through her flower photography Rosemary Calvert reveals to us details which are seldom noticed by the naked eye. Moving in close to the the centre of the flower with a macro lens and excluding everything else, she creates strong images which reveal the natural design and form which exists in nature.

Rosemary says that each time she photographs a flower she works to portray its 'personality'. With the rose it is the sensuous curves of the petals and the way they encompass each other which she emphasises, with the centre of the flower she closes in on the stigmas and stamens, working to capture the beauty of their individual design.

Emphasis on colour, pattern, form and design are part of Rosemary's style of photography and this focus runs through all her work of which flower photography is only one aspect.

She lived for some years in North America where she concentrated on wildlife and landscape photography. A number of her photographs have been commended in the Wildlife Photographer of the Year Competition and her work has been included in Photography Yearbooks since 1993, when it featured on the front cover.

Rosemary has had several exhibitions and her photographs of the natural world are frequently used in the photographic and gardening magazines. She is represented by stock agencies and her wildlife, landscape, flowers and still life images are used all over the world.

She has been a Fellow of the Royal Photographic Society since 1991. Rosemary is at present working on a book Photographing Trees, Leaves and Woodlands to be published by Fountain Press.

### Centre of purple Pansy

Canon EOS 10, 100mm macro lens, f22, 1sec,
Kodak Elite Chrome Extra

Opposite
### Centre of Passion flower
### with raindrops

Canon EOS 10, 100mm macro lens, f22, 1sec,
Fujichrome Velvia

## Centre of yellow and red Gazania

Canon EOS 10, 100mm macro lens, f22, 2sec,
Fujichrome Velvia

Opposite
## Centre of purple Freesia

Canon EOS 10, 100mm macro lens, extension
tube, f22, 1sec, Kodak Elite Chrome Extra

## Centre of Daffodil

Canon EOS 10, 100mm macro lens, extension
tube, f22, 1sec, Kodak Elite Chrome Extra

**Folded petals of deep pink Rose**

Canon EOS 10, 100mm macro lens,
f22, 3sec, Kodak Elite Chrome Extra

**Centre of pale pink Rose**

Mamiya 645, 80mm macro lens, f22, 3sec,
Fujichrome Velvia

**Folded petals of red Rose**

Mamiya 645, 80mm macro lens, f22, 1sec,
Fujichrome Provia

Opposite
**Centre of pale pink Rose**

Mamiya 645, 80mm macro lens, f22, 3sec,
Fujichrome Velvia

**Centre of red Amarylis showing stamens**

Canon EOS 10, 100mm macro lens, extension tube, f22, 1sec,
Fujichrome Velvia

Opposite

**Centre of yellow and
red Tulip**

Canon EOS 10, 100mm macro lens,
f22, 2sec, Kodak Elite Chrome Extra

**Centre of red Anemone**

Canon EOS 10, 100mm macro lens, extension
tube, f22, 1sec, Fujichrome Velvia

**Centre of pink Dahlia**
Canon EOS 10, 100mm macro lens, f22,
1/30sec, Fujichrome Velvia

**Centre of Clematis
'The President'**
Canon EOS 10, 100mm macro lens,
f22, 1/30sec, Kodak Elite Chrome Extra

Opposite
**Centre of pink Lily showing
stigma and stamens**
Canon EOS 10, 100mm macro lens, f22, 2sec, Fujichrome Velvia

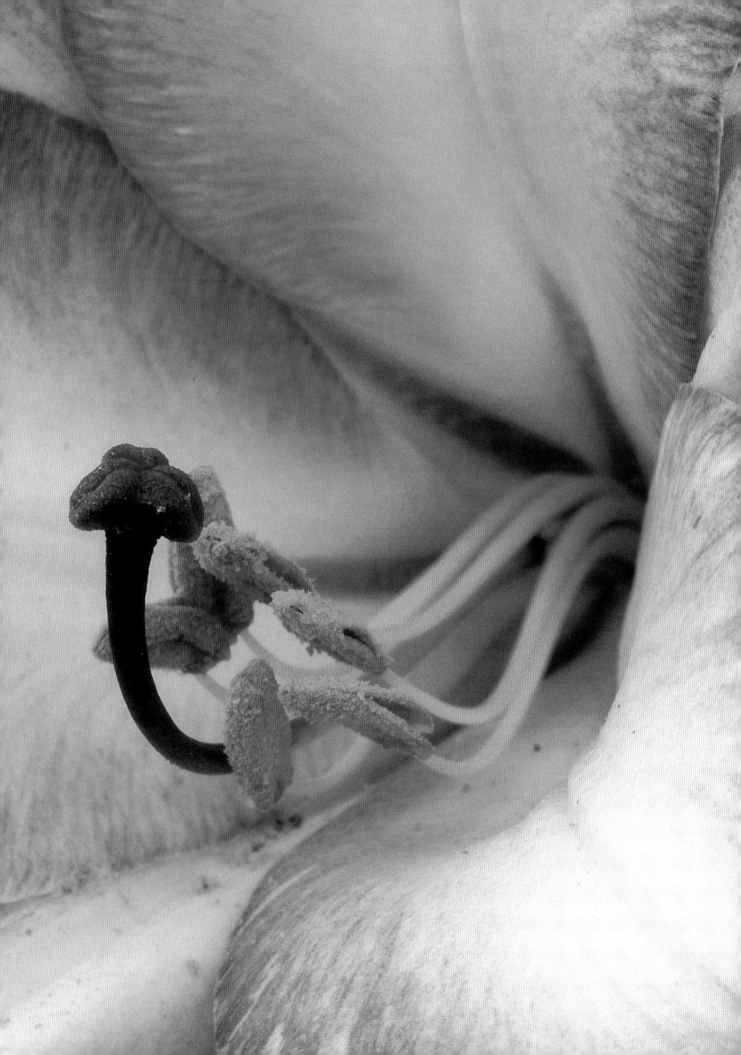

# ENCLOSURES

Photographs by
## FLORIAN STÖLLINGER

Twenty eight year old Austrian professional photographer Florian Stöllinger is that rare person to whom photography is more than a means to make a living. For Stöllinger photography is not just a technical craft but an art form. *'I am not satisfied to just realise other people's ideas, for me photography is the best method to project the images in my head into reality'* he says. Florian Stöllinger has had a comprehensive graphic education as well as investing a lot of effort in pursuing his photographic career.

The images in this portfolio are taken from his latest personal project, the creation of twelve images for a calendar. Stöllinger does not specialise in nudes but through his contacts with model agencies he was able to recruit the models he wanted. The aim of the series was to produce a symbiosis between simple geometric forms and the beauty of the human body. However he struck a major problem, the enclosures in which he wanted to place the models would have involved major expense on set-building. To avoid this expense but still realise his vision Stöllinger photographed the models on a white background and then created the enclosures digitally. This extensive use of computer manipulation also allowed him to make changes to the figures.

Stöllinger did not attempt to create erotic images, the posing of the models compliments the geometry of the enclosures, none of the models are looking into the camera and no additional props were used.

Florian Stöllinger has won the 2000 gold medal for the images featured in this portfolio by the New York Festival for international print advertising.

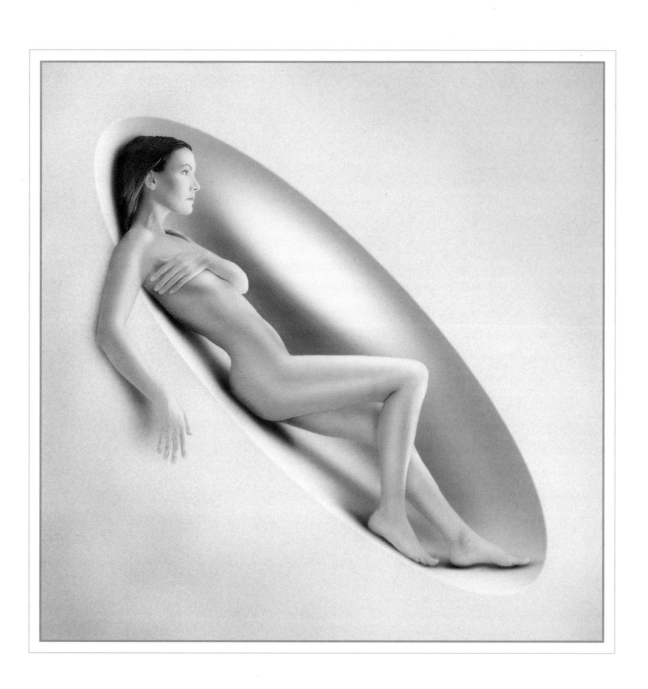

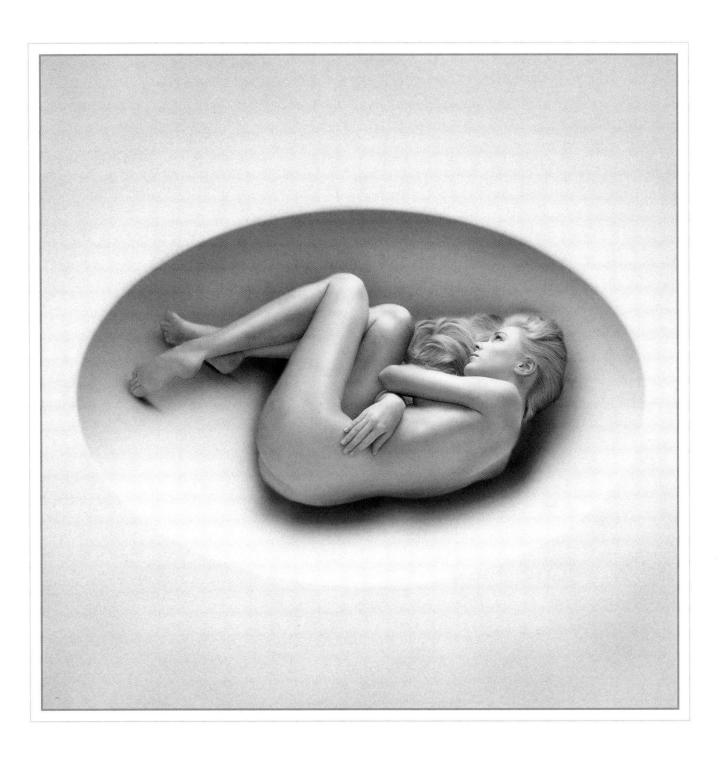

# BEYOND REALITY

Photographs by

## HANNES KUTZLER

As one of Europe's leading professionals with a series of top commissions under his belt Hannes Kutzler enjoys the challenge of combining traditional photography with digital techniques.

When still very young Kutzler decided he wanted to become an artist and by the age of nine he was painting with oils. From painting he progressed to film and produced his own experimental films whilst still at school. Later he discovered the beginning of the digital revolution in photography. Suddenly photography offered the ability to produce the fantasies he had previously created as paintings.

Kutzler decided to start by thoroughly mastering photographic technique, as he says *'Perfect technique is the basis from which to translate your own style, creativity and ideas into reality. I am not interested in special effects, but I want to attract attention, which is the advertising photographer's aim'*.

Kutzler has developed his own distinctive style, he has never imitated other photographers preferring to develop his own approach. Kutzler uses Hasselblad equipment to take his initial photographs, the final composition is then assembled and completed using an Apple Mac G3 system with Photoshop software. Kutzler says he often reduces the colour in his images to one tone, usually a cool blue, in order to emphasise the composition *'when I am able to expand the borders of reality, I know I am on the right track'*.

Success is important to Kutzler as the positive feedback confirms that his approach is the right one. He has been very lucky he says, having won major prizes including the Austrian Super Circuit and Playboy International (image on page 89)

When asked if he thinks there is a future for photography apart from digital imaging, he believes there is, as long as the quality of digital imaging isn't technically stronger than that achieved in traditional photography. He thinks the role of the professional photographer will radically change from purely recording an image to a combination of photographer and computer system operator, as he says *'A brave new world, but I love it!'*

# THE PHOTOGRAPHERS

Kevin Adlard UNITED KINGDOM 190/191
Jozef Aerts BELGIUM 161
Steve Allen UNITED KINGDOM 242/243
Nguyen Van Thu An VIETNAM 181
Helmut Anger GERMANY 222, 223
Gerald Appel UNITED STATES 92
David Aruety ISRAEL 143
Hans-Peter Banert GERMANY 156
Landi Battista ITALY 140
Pierfrancesco Baroni ITALY 184
Giuseppe Bernini ITALY 128
Rudolf Bieri SWITZERLAND 139
Stuart Black UNITED KINGDOM 230/231
G. Bradford AUSTRALIA 150
Vincent Brady IRELAND 204
Jean Brooks UNITED KINGOM 114
Nguyen Van Buu VIETNAM 168
Sophia Cheung HONG KONG 171
Luigi Degan GERMANY 118, 119
Luc Devemy GERMANY 182
John Devenport FRANCE 247
Lin Dung-Leung HONG KONG 121
Günter Eggel AUSTRIA 112
Karl Eissner GERMANY 164, 187
Javier Pedro Ferreras SPAIN 93, 135
Andrew Foley UNITED KINGDOM 206/207
Martin Gabler GERMANY 117
Heinrich Gieseler GERMANY 249
Franz Gradwohl AUSTRIA 251
Roger de Groof BELGIUM 134
Robert Gosselin BELGIUM 165
Robert M Griffith UNITED STATES 95
Lennart Gustavsson SWEDEN 113
Tan Cheng Hai SINGAPORE 180
Gregor Halbwedl AUSTRIA 111, 116
Annie Haselaars BELGIUM 160
A. van der Heiden UNITED STATES 151
Ewald Hengstschläger AUSTRIA 110
Thomas Herbrich GERMANY 219
Pål Hermansen NORWAY 105
John Hooton IRELAND 120
Long Chan Iu MACAO 157
Isidor Jecklin CANADA 93
Pavle Jovanovic YUGOSLAVIA 214/215
Teo Yong Kang SINGAPORE 178
Jonathan Kerry UNITED KINGDOM 232/233
Anton Klocker AUSTRIA 246
Evgeny Kom UKRAINE 169
Walter Kraml AUSTRIA 176
Thomas Kreher GERMANY 94
Manfred Kriegelstein GERMANY 236/237
Wim Kuiper NETHERLANDS 201
Daniel Kyndt BELGIUM 104
Wolfgang Laimer AUSTRIA 250
Avi Landau ISRAEL 154/155
Lan Sieu Lee UNITED STATES 144
K.H. Lim MALAYSIA 153
Bernd Linstaedt GERMANY 152
Tran The Long VIETNAM 154
Pun Lun HONG KONG 162
Rodrick Macmillan UNITED KINGDOM 172/173

Wolfgang Mangold AUSTRIA 106
Gianni Mantovani ITALY 216/217
Joao Avelino Marques PORTUGAL 145, 146/147
Thomas Melsheimer GERMANY 213
Dre van Mensel BELGIUM 100
Paavo Merikukka FINLAND 244/245
Hugh Milsom UNITED KINGDOM 228/229
Kiew Tin Ming SINGAPORE 163
Giulio Montini ITALY 234/235
Jesus Jaime Mota SPAIN 132/133
Jan Mrösz NETHERLANDS 240
Valter Nanut ITALY 210/211
Ewald Neffe AUSTRIA 122
Francis Nicoll BELGIUM 208
Nguyen Ninh VIETNAM 166, 167
Frankie K.H. Ng HONG KONG 170
Ta Hoang Nguyen VIETNAM 137
Tonu Noorits ESTONIA 188/189, 252/253
Hans-Joachim Of GERMANY 209
Luc Pappens BELGIUM 149
Helmut Partsch UNITED KINGDOM 183
Vicente Peiro SPAIN 238/239
Kalevi Pekkonen FINLAND 194/195
Stanko Pelc SLOVENIA 115
Erland Pillegaard DENMARK 196/197
Gerd Purrucker GERMANY 123, 126/127
Herbert Reinl GERMANY 248
Colin Roberts UNITED KINGDOM 109, 124/125
Klaus Rössner GERMANY 177
Anne Ruffell UNITED KINGDOM 202/203
Walter Scaramuzza ITALY 107
Peter Schano GERMANY 102
Klaus Schidniogrotzky GERMANY 224
Karl-Heinz Schleder GERMANY 226/227
Alexander Schneider AUSTRIA 199
Roger Schuddinck BELGIUM 200
Raoul Slater AUSTRALIA 96/97, 101
Zinovi Shegelman ISRAEL 138
Sarel van Staden SOUTH AFRICA 218, 241
Werner Staudner AUSTRIA 141
Florian Stöllinger AUSTRIA 225
Antonio Sollazzo ITALY 179
Diego Speri ITALY 185
Erich Steinerberger AUSTRIA 186
Chris Tettke GERMANY 212
John Tickner UNITED KINGDOM 142
Omero Tinagli ITALY 130/131
Pham Thi Thu VIETNAM 136
Giuseppe Tomellieri ITALY 205
Huynh Minh Tri VIETNAM 174/175
Hoang Thach Van VIETNAM 192
Alfons Vlaminckx BELGIUM 108
Veikko Wallström FINLAND 99, 129, 193
Barbara Walter AUSTRIA 198
Michael Weber GERMANY 103, 148, 158/159
Franz Wögerer AUSTRIA 91
Agustin Zambrana SPAIN 220/221

**Franz Wögerer**
AUSTRIA

Gerald Appel
UNITED STATES

**Isidor Jecklin**
CANADA

**Thomas Kreher**
GERMANY

**Robert M Griffith**
UNITED STATES

94

**Raoul Slater**
AUSTRALIA

Javier Pedro Ferreras
SPAIN

Veikko Wallström
FINLAND

**Dre van Mensel**
BELGIUM

Raoul Slater
AUSTRALIA

**Peter Schano**
GERMANY

**Michael Weber**
GERMANY

**Daniel Kyndt**
BELGIUM

**Pål Hermansen**
NORWAY

**Wolfgang Mangold**
AUSTRIA

**Walter Scaramuzza**
ITALY

**Alfons Vlaminckx**
BELGIUM

**Colin Roberts**
UNITED KINGDOM

**Ewald Hengstschläger**
AUSTRIA

**Gregor Halbwedl**
AUSTRIA

**Günter Eggel**
AUSTRIA

**Lennart Gustavsson**
SWEDEN

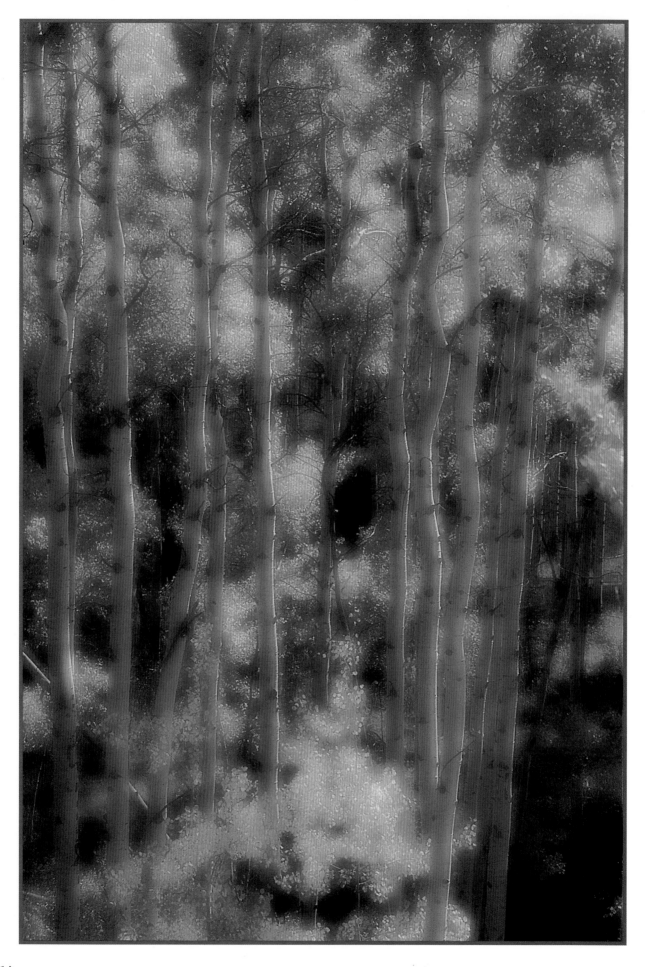

**Stanko Pelc**
SLOVENIA

**Jean Brooks**
UNITED KINGOM

**Gregor Halbwedl**
AUSTRIA

**Martin Gabler**
GERMANY

**Luigi Degan**
GERMANY

**John Hooton**
IRELAND

**Lin Dung-Leung**
HONG KONG

**Ewald Neffe**
AUSTRIA

**Gerd Purrucker**
GERMANY

OVERLEAF
**Colin Roberts**
UNITED KINGDOM

**Gerd Purrucker**
GERMANY

**Giuseppe Bernini**
ITALY

**Veikko Wallström**
FINLAND

**Omero Tinagli**
ITALY

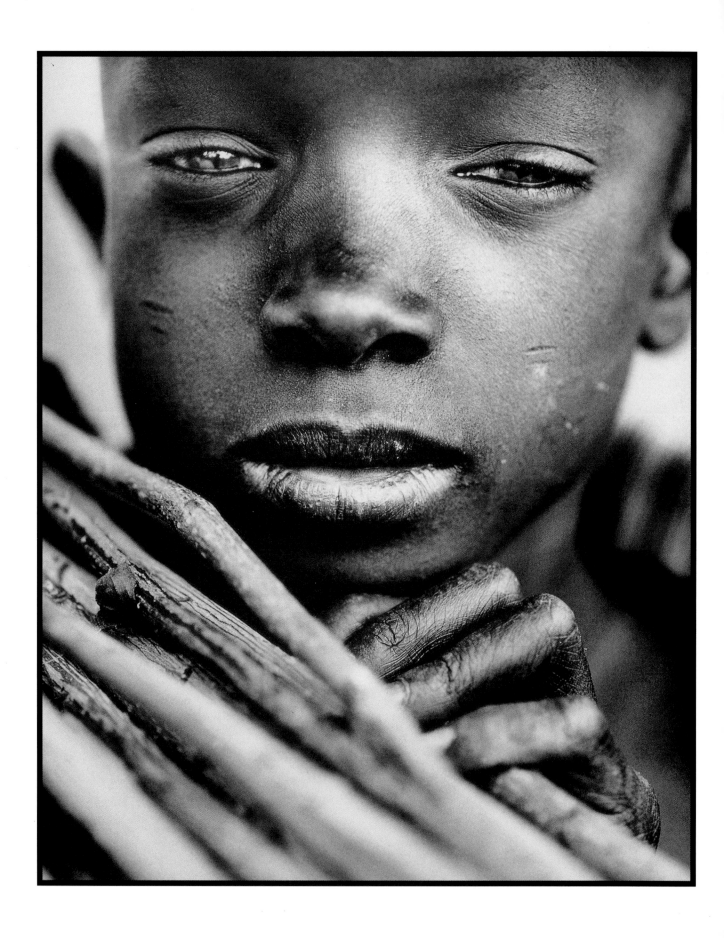

**Jesus Jaime Mota**
SPAIN

**Roger de Groof**
BELGIUM

Javier Pedro Ferreras
SPAIN

135

**Pham Thi Thu**
VIETNAM

**Ta Hoang Nguyen**
VIETNAM

**Zinovi Shegelman**
ISRAEL

**Rudolf Bieri**
SWITZERLAND

**Werner Staudner**
AUSTRIA

**Landi Battista**
ITALY

**John Tickner**
UNITED KINGDOM

**David Aruety**
ISRAEL

**Lan Sieu Lee**
UNITED STATES

**Joao Avelino Marques**
PORTUGAL

**Joao Avelino Marques**
PORTUGAL

147

**Michael Weber**
GERMANY

148

**Luc Pappens**
BELGIUM

A. van der Heiden
UNITED STATES

G. Bradford
AUSTRALIA

**Bernd Linstaedt**
GERMANY

**K.H. Lim**
MALAYSIA

**Avi Landau**
ISRAEL

**Tran The Long**
VIETNAM

**Hans-Peter Banert**
GERMANY

**Long Chan Iu**
MACAO

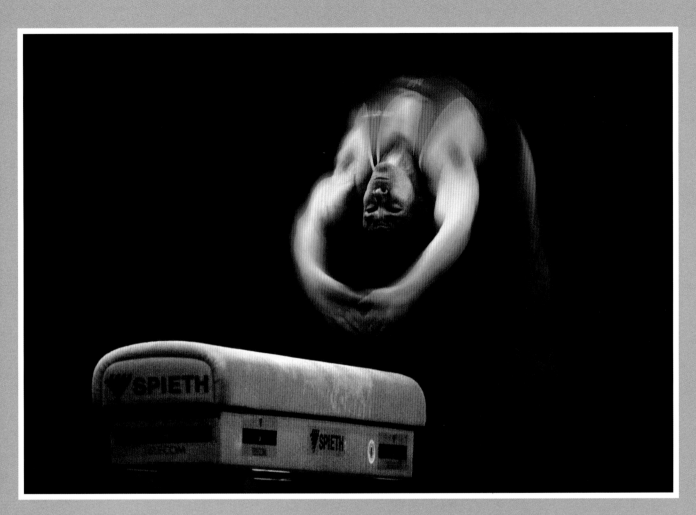

Michael Weber
GERMANY

**Annie Haselaars**
BELGIUM

Jozef Aerts
BELGIUM

161

**Pun Lun**
HONG KONG

**Kiew Tin Ming**
SINGAPORE

162

**Karl Eissner**
GERMANY

**Robert Gosselin**
BELGIUM

**Nguyen Ninh**
VIETNAM

Evgeny Kom
UKRAINE

Nguyen Van Buu
VIETNAM

169

**Frankie K.H. Ng**
HONG KONG

170

**Sophia Cheung**
HONG KONG

**Rodrick Macmillan**
UNITED KINGDOM

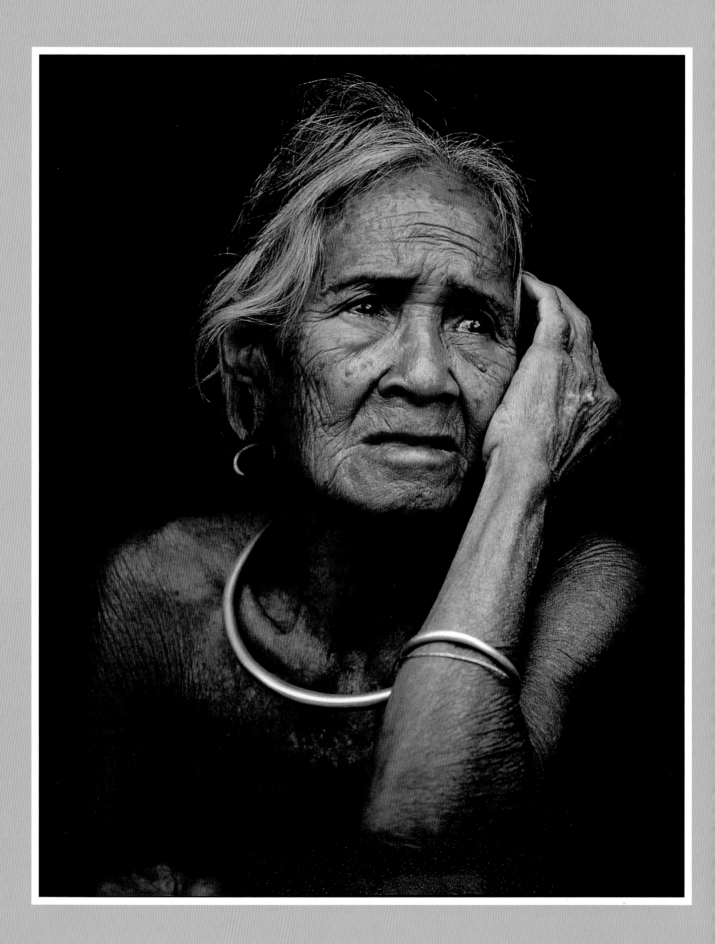

Huynh Minh Tri
VIETNAM

**Walter Kraml**
AUSTRIA

**Klaus Rössner**
GERMANY

**Antonio Sollazzo**
ITALY

**Teo Yong Kang**
SINGAPORE

179

**Nguyen Van Thu An**
VIETNAM

**Helmut Partsch**
GERMANY

**John Devenport**
UNITED KINGDOM

**Pierfrancesco Baroni**
ITALY

**Diego Speri**
ITALY

185

**Erich Steinerberger**
AUSTRIA

**Karl Eissner**
GERMANY

**Tonu Noorits**
ESTONIA

Arthur G Sticklor
UNITED STATES

**Kevin Adlard**
UNITED KINGDOM

**Hoang Thach Van**
VIETNAM

**Veikko Wallström**
FINLAND

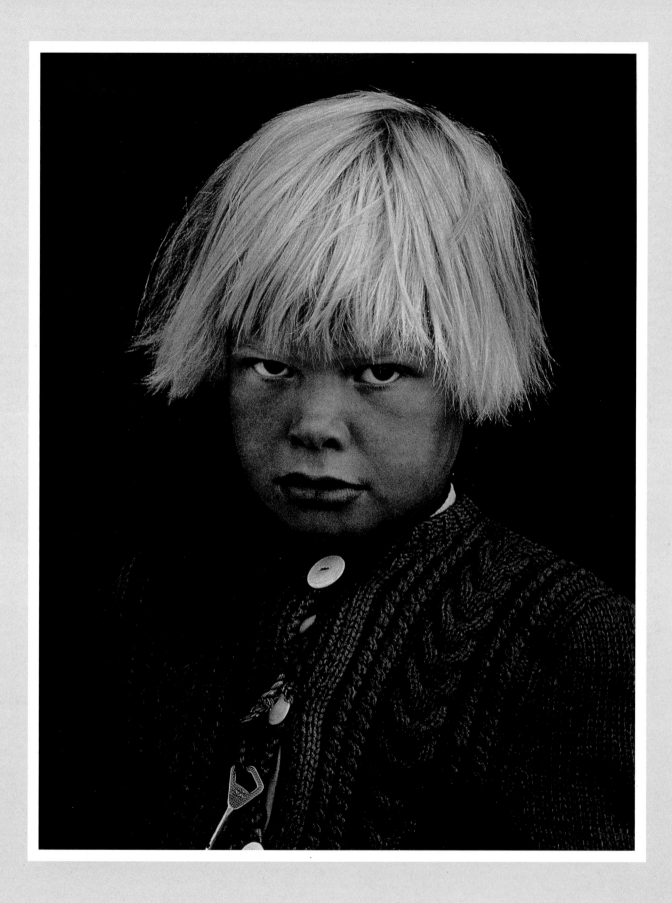

**Kalevi Pekkonen**
FINLAND

**Erland Pillegaard**
DENMARK

**Barbara Walter**
AUSTRIA

**Alexander Schneider**
AUSTRIA

**Roger Schuddinck**
BELGIUM

**Wim Kuiper**
NETHERLANDS

**Anne Ruffell**
UNITED KINGDOM

**Vincent Brady**
IRELAND

**Giuseppe Tomellieri**
ITALY

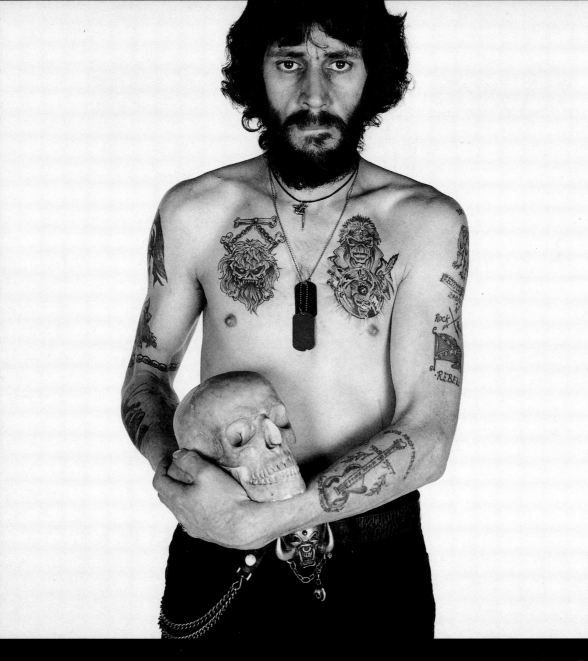

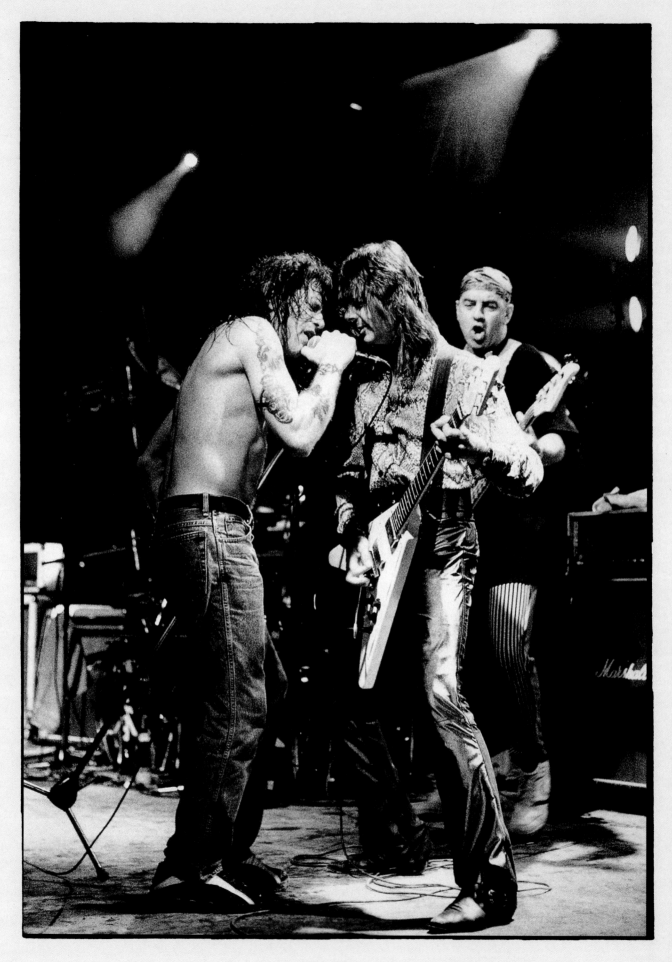

Hans-Joachim Of
GERMANY

Francis Nicoll
BELGIUM

**Valter Nanut**
ITALY

Chris Tettke
GERMANY

**Thomas Melsheimer**
GERMANY

**Pavle Jovanovic**
YUGOSLAVIA

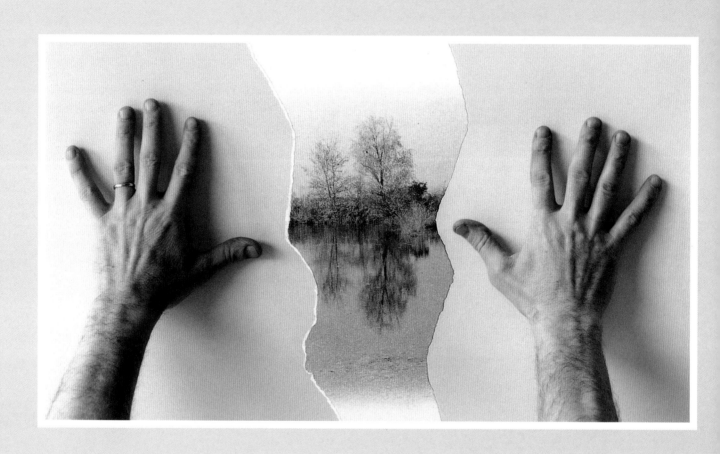

Gianni Mantovani
ITALY

Sarel van Staden
SOUTH AFRICA

Thomas Herbrich
GERMANY

**Agustin Zambrana**
SPAIN

**Helmut Anger**
GERMANY

**Klaus Schidniogrotzky**
GERMANY

**Florian Stöllinger**
AUSTRIA

**Karl-Heinz Schleder**
GERMANY

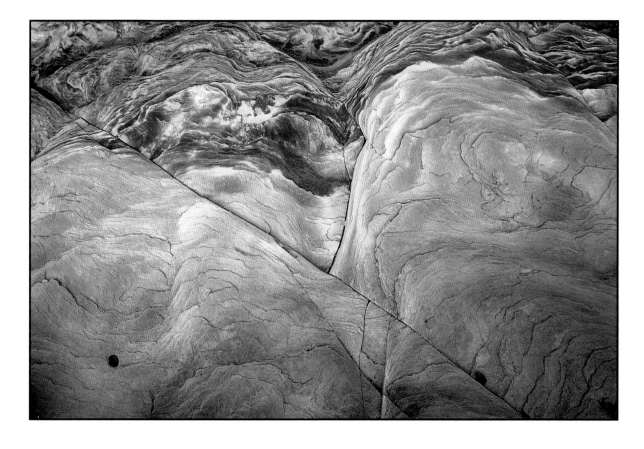

**Hugh Milsom**
UNITED KINGDOM

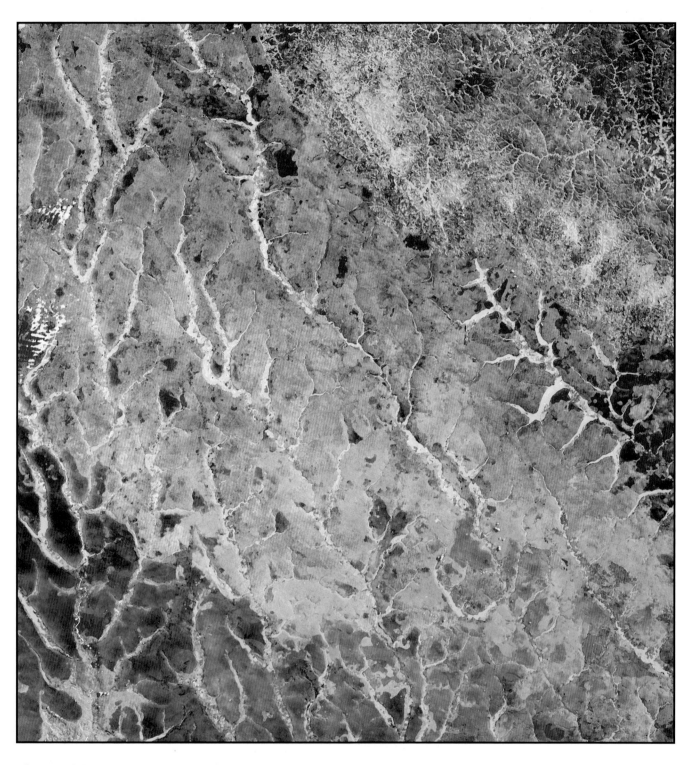

**Stuart Black**
UNITED KINGDOM

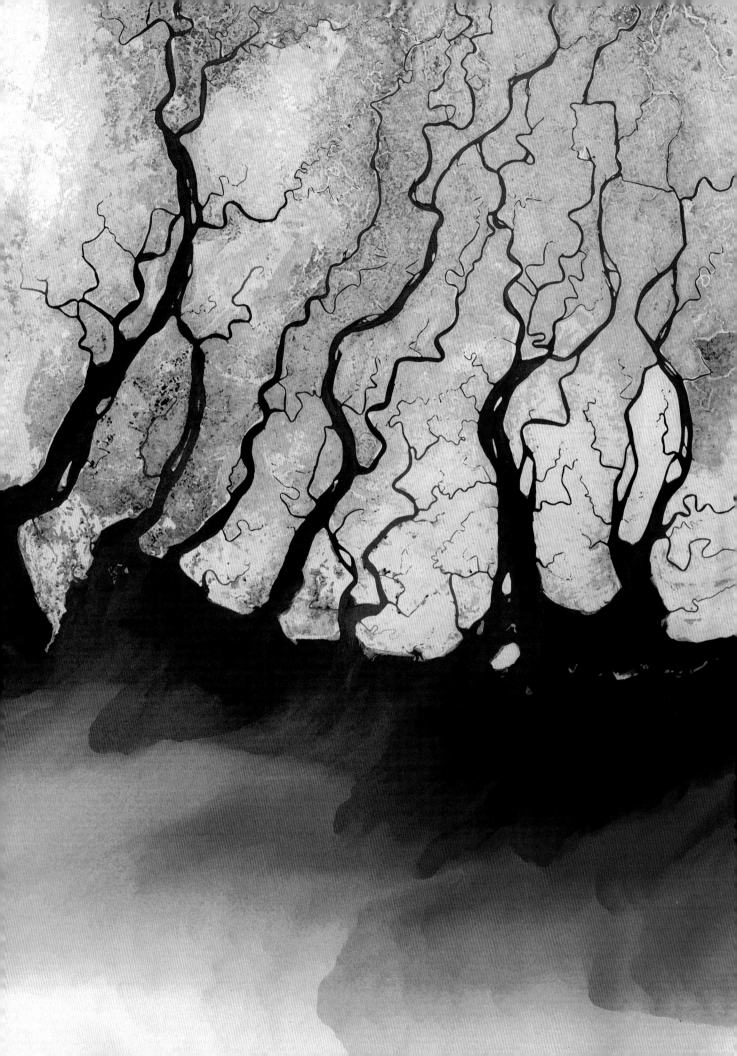

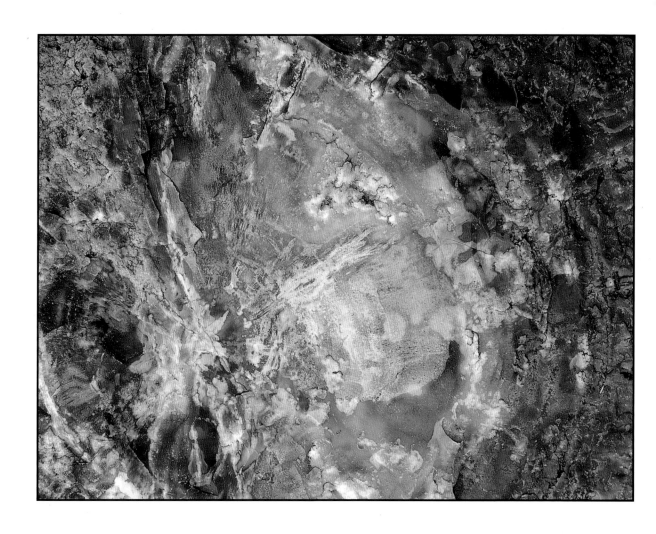

**Jonathan Kerry**
UNITED KINGDOM

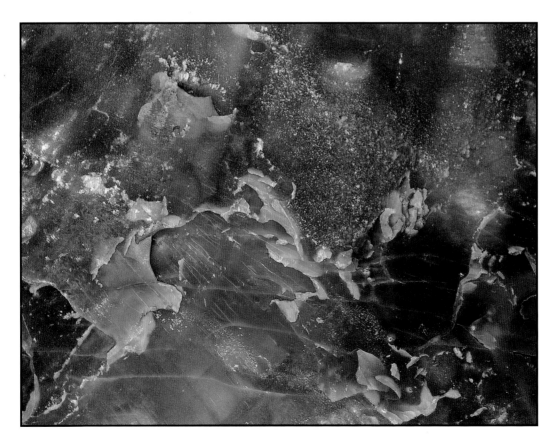

**Giulio Montini**
ITALY

Manfred Kriegelstein
GERMANY

Vicente Peiro
SPAIN

**Jan Mrösz**
NETHERLANDS

Sarel van Staden
SOUTH AFRICA

**Steve Allen**
UNITED KINGDOM

**Paavo Merikukka**
FINLAND

244

**Anton Klocker**
AUSTRIA

**Luc Devemy**
FRANCE

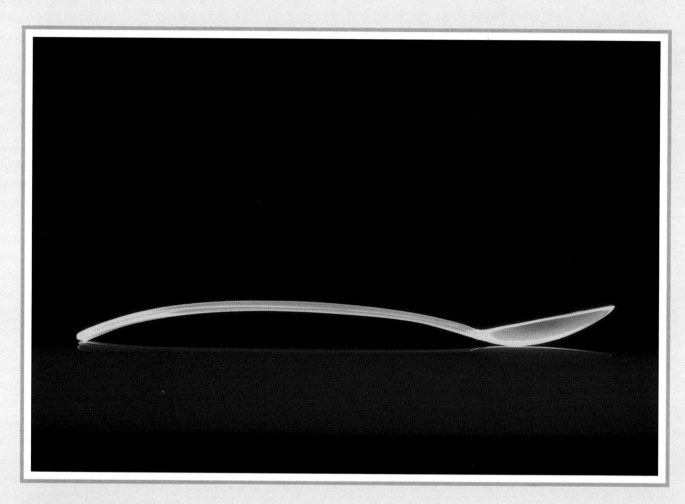

**Herbert Reinl**
GERMANY

Heinrich Gieseler
GERMANY

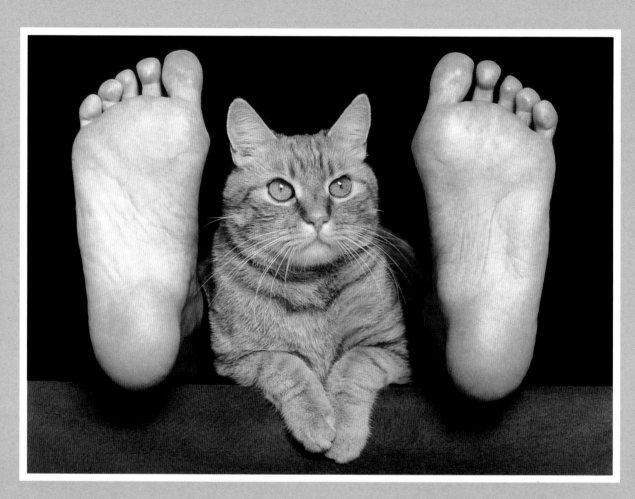

**Wolfgang Laimer**
AUSTRIA

Franz Gradwohl
AUSTRIA

**Tonu Noorits**
ESTONIA

252

**THE ART OF
CLOSE-UP PHOTOGRAPHY**
*Joseph Meehan*
ISBN 0 86343 356 1

**THE ART OF
WILDLIFE PHOTOGRAPHY**
*Fritz Pölking*
ISBN 0 86343 322 7

**THE ART & TECHNIQUE OF
UNDERWATER PHOTOGRAPHY**
*Mark Webster*
ISBN 0 86343 352 9

**THE ART OF LANDSCAPE
PHOTOGRAPHY**
*Chris Coe*
ISBN 0 86343 337 5

**WILDERNESS
PHOTOGRAPHY**
A photographic
journey through
the landscape
*Rob Beighton*
ISBN 0 86343 372 3

**INFRA-RED PHOTOGRAPHY**
**A complete workshop guide**
*Hugh Milsom*
ISBN 0 86343 373 1

**NATURE PHOTOGRAPHY**
**A studio and location
workshop**
*Arnold Wilson*
ISBN 0 86343 348 0

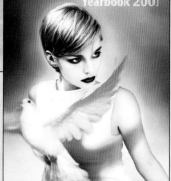

**PHOTOGRAPHY YEARBOOK 2000**
*Edited by Chris Hinterobermaier
Designed by Grant Bradford*
242 page hardback
with colour and black and white
throughout. Plus ten-page
panoramic foldout section and
Limited Edition colour hologram
ISBN 0 86343 333 2

**PHOTOGRAPHY & IMAGING
YEARBOOK 2001**
*Edited by
Chris Hinterobermaier
Designed by Grant Bradford*
ISBN 0 86343 378 2

*Also available*
**PHOTOGRAPHY
YEARBOOK 1999**
**PHOTOGRAPHY
YEARBOOK 1998**
**PHOTOGRAPHY
YEARBOOK 1997**

**Larry Bartlett's
BLACK & WHITE
Photographic Printing Workshop**
ISBN 0 86343 366 9

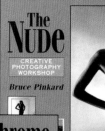

**BEYOND
MONOCHROME
A Fine Art
Printing Workshop**
*Tony Worobiec
& Ray Spence*
ISBN 0 86343 313 8

**THE NUDE
Creative
Photography
Workshop**
*Bruce Pinkard*
ISBN 0 86343 39

**CREATIVE ELEMENTS
Landscape Photography – Darkroom
Techniques**
*Eddie Ephraums*
ISBN 0 86343 397 9

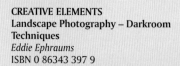

**Photographing BUTTERFLIES AND OTHER INSECTS**
Paul Hicks
ISBN 0 86343 332 4

**MARA-SERENGETI**
A Photographer's Paradise
*Jonathan & Angela Scott*
ISBN 0 86343 398 7

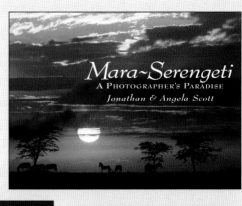

**Photographing BIRDS IN THE WILD**
Paul Hicks
ISBN 0 86343 357 X

**Jonathan Scott's Safari Guide to East African Birds**
*Revised and updated by Angela Scott*
ISBN 0 86343 318 9

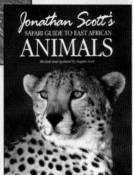

**Photographing ANIMALS IN THE WILD**
Andy Rouse
ISBN 0 86343 362 6

**Jonathan Scott's Safari Guide to East African Animals**
*Revised and updated by Angela Scott*
ISBN 0 86343 323 5

**VENICE**
Reflections of a City
*Francisco Hidalgo*
ISBN 0 86343 304 9

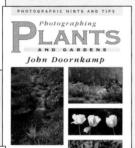

**Photographing PLANTS AND GARDENS**
John Doornkamp
ISBN 0 86343 363 4

**THE COMPLETE PHOTOGRAPHER**
A Complete Practical Guide to Every Aspect of Photography
*Ron Spillman*
ISBN 0 86343 342 X

**WILDLIFE PHOTOGRAPHER OF THE YEAR PORTFOLIO NINE**
ISBN 0 86343 383 3

**A TIGER'S TALE**
The Indian Tiger's Struggle for Survival in the Wild
*Anup & Manoj Shah*
ISBN 0 86343 391 X

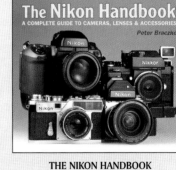

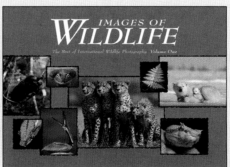

**THE REPRODUCTION OF COLOUR**
*Dr. R.W.G. Hunt*
ISBN 0 86343 368 5

**THE NIKON HANDBOOK**
A Complete Guide to Cameras, Lenses & Accessories
*Peter Braczko*
ISBN 0 86343 383 9

**IMAGES OF WILDLIFE**
The Best of International Wildlife Photography
*Volume One Edited by Harry Ricketts*
ISBN 0 86343 367 7

**MEASURING COLOUR**
*Dr. R.W.G. Hunt*
ISBN 0 86343 387 1

**FOUNTAIN PRESS**
Newpro UK Limited, Old Sawmills Road, Faringdon, Oxon SN7 7DS England
Telephone: 01367 242411 Fax: 01367 241124
E-mail: sales@newprouk.co.uk

# 10. *HASSELBLAD* AUSTRIAN SUPER CIRCUIT

The largest annual salon of photography

## LET US SEE YOUR EYECATCHERS ....

## .... AND WIN

US$ 30.000 cash money...

...plus a *HASSELBLAD* Xpan...

...plus a *HASSELBLAD* 503 CW

And get a 200 page catalogue, containing the 400 best entries

Closing date: August 6th 2001

INFORMATIONS AND ENTRY FORMS ARE AVAILABLE AT:

http://fly.to/supercircuit or email to austriansupercircuit@netway.at
*or mail to Hasselblad Austrian Super Circuit,* Postfach 364, A-4010 Linz, Austria

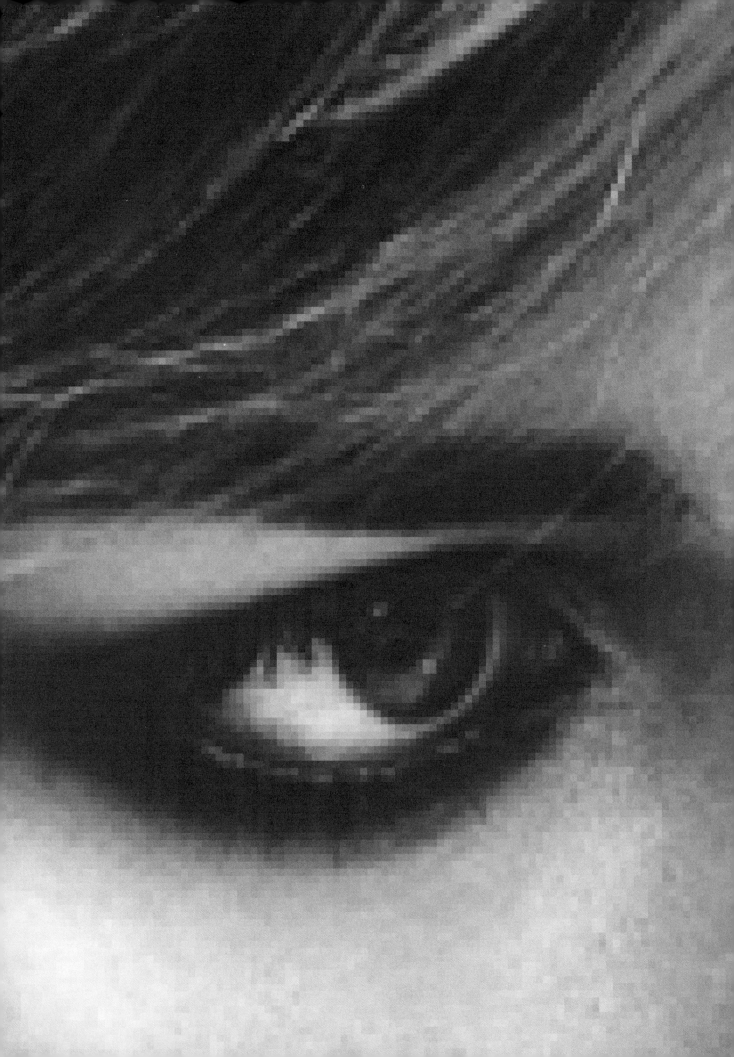